I0004599

Adobe Illustrator Ai CC 2015: The New and Enhanced Features

Introduction

Adobe Illustrator Ai CC 2015 is an improved version of Adobe Illustrator with new features that allow you to create logos, sketches, and complex illustrations with ease. You can create graphic designs for mobiles, web and print as well as interactive and video graphics. The new version is fast and provides an easy access to the Adobe Creative Cloud and its Libraries and Stock photos. The new and improved graphic designing capability of Adobe Illustrator Ai CC 2015 gives designers the ability to translate their creativity into productive designs more efficiently.

1. ADOBE STOCK INSIDE ILLUSTRATOR

Being a part of Adobe Creative Cloud, Adobe Illustrator Ai CC 2015 has access to the millions of assets available in the Adobe Stock. You can search high-quality illustrations, images and vectors from the search field on Adobe Stock website or from the search field in Illustrator and download or purchase them.

2. DIRECT IMAGE PLACEMENT

Adobe illustrator Ai CC 2015 has full integration with Adobe Stock. You can search an asset such as an image or a vector and download it to your desktop or CC library. On top of that, you can also open and place that asset directly in your design.

3. STOCK IMAGES IN-APP PURCHASE

This is one of the latest features introduced in the Adobe Illustrator Ai 2015. Now, you can buy the asset you want right from the Illustrator. Through CC Libraries Panel, search for an image from Adobe Stock and place it in your document. Right there, you will find a Shopping Cart icon. Click it to initiate a purchase. Thus, you don't need to leave your project to buy the images you want.

4. BETTER COLLABORATION WITH LIBRARIES

Illustrator Ai CC 2015 gives members access to the Creative Cloud Libraries for read-only. This means that the members can access the libraries but cannot delete or edit them. These enhanced Libraries afford more control and collaboration among users and a better integration with Adobe Stock estimated to have more than 50 million assets to choose from.

5. UPDATED LIBRARIES PANEL

The Libraries Panel is bigger with faster search filters that let you search according to different themes. The icons are also bigger that helps you identify the Adobe assets that are licensed.

6. ENHANCED CREATIVE CLOUD LIBRARIES

Illustrator lets you use the enhanced Creative Cloud Libraries for accessing and sharing you assets produced through Illustrator across different devices and with different users. With Illustrator Ai CC 2015, keep a track of assets that you use as brand identity, video clips, specific icons for web layout, color themes and frequently used brushes and swatches. You can even search the enhanced libraries for color groups, swatches and even text styles to depict your creativity through text. This gives you enhanced creative control on your designs.

7. EDIT ONCE, UPDATE EVERYWHERE

Adobe illustrator's collaboration with the enhanced CC Libraries gives a lot of functional flexibility to the Illustrator user with ease and speed. All the assets in the Libraries are linked together. Now if you change a design or a layout for a project, your team members get that updated file automatically. Thus, everything stays up-to-date with the latest edits available across the board.

8. DESIGN PORTABILIY

The enhanced collaboration with CC Libraries allows you to use your Illustrator from your PC, tablet or any other device without having to worry about copying data or keeping duplicate files on each device to work with. That's a big advantage for clutter-free seamless workflow. Open any device, access your Library files in Illustrator and unleash your creativity.

9. FAST EXPORT OF ASSETS AND ARTBOARDS

You can select a single asset such as an image or illustration or choose an entire artboard to export for your use. Similarly, you can choose multiple assets from different artboards. With one click you can change their size, format or resolution to match the intended purpose such as screen, icon or web.

10. CREATE MULTIPLE ARTBOARDS

Now you can set up multiple artboards within the Illustrator. Go to windows > Artboards within the Illustrator to manage different artboards through Artboards panel. With this panel you can add or remove artboards, reorder or rearrange them or

change their names. You can also specify presets for Artboard
size and their relative positions.

11. LIVE SHAPES

Most of the Shape tools in Illustrator are live which means that
they can be transformed easily and quickly. Now you can adjust
the traditional vector shapes dynamically to modify them
according to your creative need. You don't need to apply
special effects to get the desired shapes and can do so
interactively with ease. If you do not like the changes, you
can reset through the Transform panel.

12. EASY TRANSFORM

Working with live shapes is easier now due to a clutter-free
working space around the shape. The shape bounding box is
simpler now and provides a consistent visual experience. When
you scale a shape to a smaller size, the bounding box
automatically disappears for a more clear view.

13. POLYGON TRANSFORM

In case of non-uniform scaling, polygons retain their live properties. The radius widget is not set at 90 degree angle by default anymore. If you modify a polygon such as scale, shear or reshape it, you have the option to make your polygon uniform by making its sides equal in length.

14. COMPLEX LIVE SHAPE COMPONENTS

When you create complex shapes by using your live shapes, the layers panel shows every live shape as a different object in the layers panel. Thus when you want to delete or transform a shape, you can select and modify it easily by selecting the object it represents. You can also select all the objects of the same shape by using Select Menu option where a new menu option for selecting same shapes has been added. Go to Select > Same > Shape and this will select all live shape objects of the same kind.

15. LIVE CORNERS

In the live shapes, when you select a corner anchor point, a Live Corner Widget appears next to the corner point. You can select several corner anchor points in a simple path or throughout your artwork. The widget allows you to change the shape of the corner. You can choose from round, inverted round or chamfer shapes. You can also change other settings like the style, radius and type of curves from the Corners Dialog.

16. ADOBE PORTFOLIO

New Adobe Portfolio lets you showcase your work directly through Illustrator Ai CC 2015. With Portfolio you can also create custom landing pages to show off your illustrations and designs. You can also create custom pages for your Portfolio to connect with the viewers in a personalized way.

17. START WORKSPACE

Start Workspace gives you an easy access to different functionalities of Illustrator. From your Start Workspace, all the Libraries and Starter Templates are a click away. You can easily open your recently used files from this workspace as well. The Start Workspace is displayed when you launch the Illustrator or close the Illustrator documents that you've been working on. If you don't want this new Start Workspace, you can revert to the old Open Dialog by typing Ctrl/Cmd + O.

18. RECENT FILES WORKSPACE

Recent Files Workspace is displayed when you have an open document in Illustrator. In this workspace you can view the recent files that you've been working on. If you cannot see your recent files in the workspace, go to Preferences and tick the checkbox for Show Recent Files workspace when opening a file.

19. SHAPER TOOL

Shaper is an excellent tool in the Illustrator that gives you a lot of creative freedom. It converts your natural gestures into live shapes on which other complex shapes can be built. This ease and freedom lets you invest your thoughts more on the design than on how to design. The perfectly geometric shapes produced by shaper tool can be used just like regular shapes in Illustrator. You can transform them, join them, delete them or fill them as you like. Whatever you do with these shapes, each component stays fully editable.

20. SHAPE BUILDER FREE-FORM MODE

Previously, the shape builder tool used linear feedback for Subtract and Merge options but now the default mode for shape builder to work is free-form mode. Create a shape that has overlapping components for applying shape builder tool. Now by selection tool, select the paths that you need to merge. Select the shape builder tool. It's in merge mode by default. Now drag the shape builder tool along the region to merge and a new shape with merged boundaries is made. If you don't want to use this free-form mode, you can revert back to straight line feedback through option dialog for the tool.

21. DYNAMIC SYMBOLS

Dynamic symbols offer a great functionality to Illustrator users. They offer a design hierarchy in which a shape is assigned the role of Master. This Master Symbol can be changed to have different characteristics such as color, fill or opacity or you can mirror, rotate, skew or scale them. Now the underlying design symbol is same for all the Child Symbols but they have their own unique appearances as well. For example, you can choose a shirt design as the Master Symbol and its depiction in various colors and sizes are the variable instances for master design. Now if you want to change the design of the shirt, all you need is to alter the design of the Master Symbol.

All the lower level designs will show the altered master design with their own preferences of color and size.

22.   SMART GUIDES

Smart Guides in Illustrator Ai CC 2015 gives you the new ability to align and position the objects through guidelines. Follow hints and guides offered by tools to use them optimally. You can now draw perfect shapes without using modifiers or pressing down special control keys. Draw, move and align shapes or extend or draw a line along the trajectory used by another object using guidelines and hints from the Illustrator.

23.   SVG EXPORT

Adobe Illustrator Ai CC 2015 has incorporated SVG export feature so that you can get SVG files that are optimized for web. Go to File > Export > SVG to export individual objects in SVG format ideal for web and screen designs. The SVG code by Illustrator is modern and clean and you have the liberty to choose individual objects instead of complete artboard for export. SVG codes are crucial to UX designers and web designers to create vector based graphics that can be displayed on all screens such as HiDPI display screens.

24. TOUCH WORKSPACE

Adobe Illustrator 2015 has a new Touch Workspace designed
primarily for windows 8 tablet. You can access important tools
like Shaper Tool, Smart Guides and Live Shapes to create and
edit your designs. The Libraries Panel in Touch Workspace lets
you access your assets quickly. All the functionalities are
achieved by pressure sensitive pen and touch sensitivity. The
Touch Workspace HP Sprout platform that lets you draw and edit
with Sprout Touch mat and get the preview of your work on
Sprout's vertical screen. Touch workspace now has a new mobile-
to-desktop facility that supports Android as well.

25. IMAGE PLACEMENT AND SELECTION

Touch Workspace allows you to place images in raster format. To
select an object in the touch workspace, tap the Selection tool
in the tools panel. Now drag your finger over the objects to
choose or use the pen. You can also use Add/Subtract button
from the Selection Tool Options menu to select a group of
objects or add or remove an object from the group you've already
selected.

26. JOIN TOOL

Join tool is a handy tool for the paths that cross over or overlap or the ends that don't touch. You can use join tool to join the open ends of a path or remove the parts that are not wanted. Just select the join tool and erase the segments that need to be deleted, just like you would use an average eraser. Similarly, join the paths that don't meet by scrubbing the tool on the place where you want the path to meet and the open ends will extend to meet in a corner point.

27. CIRCLE CREATION

Now you can draw circles and other regular shapes without using any modifier key. In the Touch Workspace, go to Tools Panel and select Ellipse tool. Select 'Draw from Center' and also select 'constraint proportions' from Tool Options Panel. These two options will ensure that you get a perfect proportional circle around the point where you tap to draw the circle. Now tap the screen and drag on your artboard to make a circle as big as you like.

28. TOUCH ZOOM AND PAN

With touch workspace, pan and zoom your documents fast and easy with your finger.

- Pinch out the screen using your two fingers to zoom in.
- Pinch in the screen using your two fingers to zoom out.
- Tap and drag with your two fingers to pan the screen in Illustrator.

29. DOCUMENT VIEW PANEL

The Document View Panel in Touch Workspace allows you many different options for document views. For example, you can choose to fit all your artboards in the workspace window or choose to fit only the active artboard. Similarly, you can tap with your finger to choose to see your document in its actual size.

30. CURVATURE TOOL TOUCH WORKSPACE

Using Curvature tool in the Touch workspace is easy and smooth. Tap to mark the points for the curve you want and then let the curvature tool flex the path around these points in real time. To make corner points for straight lines, tap twice/double-tap. To make changes in the path you've just created, use the same

tool and tap some new points along the path. Now drag the
existing points to the new adjusted points.

31. RUBBER-BANDING PREFERENCES

Previously the rubber-banding preferences for Curvature and Pen
tools were the same and one couldn't be changed alone. This
posed many functional restrictions for Illustrator users.
Therefore, in Adobe 2105 you can change the preferences for the
Curvature tool independent of the Pen tool.

32. JOINING TWO PATHS

Previously, the curvature tool of Illustrator only worked with
the active path. This restricted design creation and limited
creative production of the design. Now you can join an inactive
path and can work with it as well.

33. CURVATURE TOOL DIRECTION

The curvature tool used to have fixed direction, meaning by, you
could only draw from one end of the shape. Even if you wanted
to select or deselect a path, you could do so in one direction
only. But now you can select which end of the path you want to
work with. If you want to work from the other end-point,
deselect the active point by pressing ESC and then move the end-

point slightly. Now you can start drawing the same path from
the opposite end.

34. DISTRIBUTE OPTIONS IN ALIGN PANEL

The Align panel in Adobe Illustrator Ai CC 2015 has incorporated
the distribute options to give you more creative flexibility.
You can use the popular distribute options right from the Align
Panel in Touch Workspace. Illustrator uses the axis you specify
to align or distribute the selected objects around it. The axis
can be object edges or the anchor points. Based on the object's
path, Illustrator calculates the values for alignment and
distribution.

35. TOOL RESET WHILE SWITCHING

In Touch Workspace, you can easily toggle between different
tools for example switching from Shape Tools to Shape Builder.
Now let's say if you've selected 'Draw from Center' for the
Shape Tool and 'Merge and Subtract' mode in Shape Builder. When
you switch between the two tools while working intently on your
design, you forget what setting for the other tool was. This
leads to a lot of frustration, time loss, and less productivity.

To overcome this problem, Illustrator resets the tool settings
to default whenever you switch between tools in Touch Workspace.

36. FLIP BUTTONS FOR VARIABLE WIDTH

Now you can apply variable-width to paths by using Stroke
Options in Touch workspace. This helps them look organic.
Based on an undefined direction, the variable-width profile
literally means of variable width i.e. one end thicker than the
other. Flip buttons give more control to these profiles by
using Flip buttons to adjust the placement and other attributes.

37. FLIP FUNCTIONALITY

Flip functionality is very useful in Illustrator as it affords a
lot of flexibility to use the designs that you've already made.
Flip your designs across an axis, e.g. horizontal or vertical
axis. You may also choose a freeform axis or an imaginary line
to flip the entire design. You may choose to flip the pattern
only or may flip the entire object.

38. NAVIGATOR PANEL

Use thumbnail display to change the view of your artwork from
the Navigation Panel. The proxy view area bounded by a

colourful line shows the area viewable at that time. You can personalize the Navigator Panel to meet your preferences. For example, change the color of the Proxy View Area, display the artwork outside the boundary of artboard, or change the dashed lines to solid ones.

39. MULTIPLE VIEWS

You can open and save multiple views for the same document in Illustrator. This helps you to set a separate setting for each view for the same document. For example, set one view with high magnification for detailing, while create another one with less magnification for seeing all the objects at a glance. You can create about 25 views for a single document and save the views along with the document. Give each view a separate name to identify them. To display all the views of a document simultaneously, you need to open multiple windows, a separate window for each view.

40. PENCIL TOOL: AUTO-CLOSE CONTROL

Now you can choose whether you want Pencil Tool to Auto-Close a path or not. When you draw with your pencil tool in Illustrator and two ends of a path are near (based on certain minimum number of pixels), the cursor indicates 'path-close icon'. Now if you release the pencil tool, Illustrator closes the path automatically for you. This feature was introduced in the release of 2014 and was appreciated by a large group of Users. However, many craved for more control, so now in Illustrator 2015 you can toggle the Pencil Tool Auto-Close feature on and off as you wish.

41. FLARE TOOL

The Flare Tool lets you draw objects with rings, rays or an object with a bright center like a lens flare. Flares have two handles, a center handle and an end handle. The flare path begins from the center handle which is the brightest spot and it ends at the end handle. Change the length and the direction of the flare through these handles.

42. HEXADECIMAL COPY/PASTING

The Hex field in Color Panel has just gone smart in Adobe Illustrator Ai CC 2015. When you copy hexadecimal values from other applications, there are many other hidden characters and the notorious # tag that gets copied as well. Now when you paste this number in your Hex field, the application doesn't accept it. This is because the Hex field only accepts the

precise hexadecimal value without anything appended to it. The
smart Hex field in Illustrator now has the ability to separate
the actual value from all the other appended characters. So now
you don't need to copy and paste repeatedly to get your hex
value right.

43. SWATCHES AS COLOR STOP

Swatch colors are often used as color stops. You must have
experienced that when you double click the Color Stop, you
cannot identify the swatch that was used to define it. This is
no longer a problem because now when you double click the Color
Stop, the swatch is highlighted by the Illustrator. Also, the
color swatch in question retains all the information.

44. INSPIRATION ON THE GO

Adobe Illustrator boasts the ability to let you gather and use
inspiration on the go. With its app support use your iPhone,
iPad, or Android phone to turn any inspiration into an asset.
Due to app integration, Illustrator lets you extract information
from the surroundings, save it in the CC Libraries and use it as
an asset for production in Illustrator. You can pull out

shapes, vector images, color themes or create brushes out of the information you capture.

45. 10x FASTER ZOOM, PAN AND SCROLL

Due to Mercury Performance System enhancements, now you can Zoom, Scroll and Pan 10 times faster in Illustrator. The new animated Zoom allows you to zoom in and out quickly with the flick of your finger. While using mouse, you can click and hold a point and zoom in dynamically. This time saving capability is available for both windows and Mac users.

46. 10x GREATER ZOOM MAGNIFICATION

Not only speed but the zoom magnification has also increased 10 times in Illustrator 2015. Now you can zoom up to 64,000 % instead of the previous limit of 6,400%. The greater magnification lets you work with high precision and accuracy. You can make exact edits and can include finest details.

47. PRINT TILING

If you want to print your artboard on paper, Illustrator prints each artwork on a single paper by default. But if your artwork is larger and cannot fit on a single sheet of paper, then you can do Print Tiling to print it on multiple sheets of paper. For Print Tiling choose tiling option from print options. The program numbers the papers for your reference only but doesn't print them.

48. SAFE MODE

The safe mode provides you the ability to troubleshoot your program by giving you access to the interface and diagnosis report. With Safe Mode feature, you can launch your Illustrator even if there is a fatal error due to corrupt files, incorrect drivers, outdated plugins or any other crash-inducing problem in the system. The application diagnoses the cause of error, isolates the faulty files, disable them and launch the Illustrator in Safe Mode. Then the program gives you an opportunity to resolve the issues by providing you with the crash report and the ways to fix it. Fix all the issues, mark them resolved and relaunch Illustrator. If the issues are resolved, application will launch in Normal Mode now.

49. DATE RECOVERY

There are moments of indulgence when you are taken over by your creative spur and forget to save your open projects periodically as you design. Then all of a sudden your Illustrator shuts down automatically without allowing you to save your work. This improper shutdown may be due to power outage, Illustrator crashing or Operating System errors. Whatever the reason, it's a cause of much stress for the users due to loss of hard work. Now with Adobe Illustrator Ai CC 2015, just relaunch the program and you'll be able to restore all your work. The illustrator will guide you to fix the cause if the failure was due to errors in Illustrator.

50. GPU PERFORMANCE

Illustrator Ai CC 2015 leverages the power of GPU in a better way to process and submit content. To compute and render the content on a graphic processor, each art type is rewritten making it faster to render artwork while scrolling, panning, or zooming. This enhanced feature is now available for Macs too.